U.S. Military Forces

U.S. MARINES

JULIA GARSTECKI

BLACK RABBIT BOOKS

Bolt is published by Black Rabbit Books
P.O. Box 3263, Mankato, Minnesota, 56002.
www.blackrabbitbooks.com

Jennifer Besel, editor; Michael Sellner, interior designer;
Catherine Cates, cover designer; Omay Ayres, photo researcher

Library of Congress Cataloging-in-Publication Data
Names: Garstecki, Julia, author.
Title: U.S. Marines / by Julia Garstecki.
Description: Mankato, Minnesota : Black Rabbit Books, [2021]
Series: Bolt. U.S. military forces | Includes bibliographical references and index.
Audience: Grades 4-6 | Audience: Ages 8-12
Summary: "Learn about the powerful soldiers who make up the U.S. Marines, including what they do and the training it takes to become one"— Provided by publisher.
Identifiers: LCCN 2019037854 (print) | LCCN 2019037855 (ebook)
ISBN 9781623102999 (hardcover) | ISBN 9781644663950 (paperback) |
ISBN 9781623103934 (ebook)
Subjects: LCSH: United States. Marine Corps—Juvenile literature. | Marines—United States—Juvenile literature.
Classification: LCC VE23 .G378 2021 (print) | LCC VE23 (ebook)
DDC 359.9/60973—dc23
LC record available at https://lccn.loc.gov/2019037854
LC ebook record available at https://lccn.loc.gov/2019037855

Image Credits

24thmeu.marines.mil: Sgt. Alex Sauceda/U.S. Marine Corps, 22; 26thmeu.marines.mil: Staff Sgt. Dengrier M. Baez/U.S. Marine Corps, 3; Alamy: Alex Edelman/CNP /MediaPunch, 16 (tl); APFootage, 7; Conner Flecks, 6; archive.defense.gov: Sgt. Emmanuel Ramos/U.S. Marines, 4–5; defenceimagery.mod.uk: Defence Imagery, 24–25; defense.gov: Lance Cpl. Devon Burton/U.S. Marine Corps, 10–11; Petty Officer 1st Class Elizabeth Merriam/U.S. Navy, 23 (t); Staff Sgt. Kenneth Norman/U.S. Marine Corps, 9 (phase 3); U.S. Air Force, 26 (Hornet & Harrier); U.S. Marine Corps, 23 (b), 31; dod.defense.gov: Cpl. Alexander Sturdivant, Cover (main); U.S. Navy Petty Officer 1st Class Dominique A. Pineiro/D.o.D., 17 (br); dodlive.mil: Cpl. Austin Long/US Marine Corps, 21; Magnum Photos: Moises Saman, 16–17 (main); marines.mil: Conner Flecks, 1, 6; Lance Cpl. Tanner D. Lambert/U.S. Marine Corps, 9 (phase 2); U.S. Marine Corps, 15 (b), 27 (Osprey & Lightning), 28; mcrdsd.marines.mil: Lance Cpl. Pedro Cardenas/U.S. Marine Corps, 9 (phase 1 & 4); navy.mil: Banuelos RodriguezU.S. Navy, 15 (t); Petty Officer 1st Class Tom Ouellette/U.S. Navy, 18; pacom.mil: Lance Cpl. Tanner Lambert/U.S. Marine Corps, 12, 32; Shutterstock: 19srb81, 9 (bkgd); Neuevector, Cover (wings); usni.org: USNI News, 17 (bl); Every effort has been made to contact copyright holders for material reproduced in this book. Any omissions will be rectified in subsequent printings if notice is given to the publisher.

Contents

CHAPTER 1

To Protect and Serve

It was 2004. Fallujah, Iraq, was a battleground. **Insurgents** had taken control of the city. The United States brought in the Marines. Their job was to take back the city.

The enemies placed bombs throughout the city. They also hid in buildings, ready to shoot. But the Marines were ready. They went door to door. They **disarmed** bombs. And they pushed out the enemy.

Important Roles

Fighting enemies is the main job of the U.S. Marine Corps. Members are highly trained soldiers. They keep the United States safe.

Marines have other important jobs too. They protect U.S. **citizens** and buildings all over the world. They even **transport** the president.

CHAPTER 2

Training

Marines go through a lot of training. Every soldier starts with boot camp. This basic training lasts 13 weeks. **Recruits** get very little sleep. They must prove they are strong and smart enough to be Marines. Boot camp has four phases.

Phase 1

take strength test

learn Corps values of honor, courage, and commitment

learn close combat

Phase 2

do hours of target practice

fire live rounds

Phase 3

go through the Crucible test

learn combat survival

Phase 4

final inspections

graduation

THE CRUCIBLE
By the Numbers

The Crucible is a test all Marines must pass. It is stressful and difficult. Recruits face long marches and combat courses. They must work together to succeed.

54 HOURS
total time the event takes

2
number of meals they get

6 HOURS
amount of sleep recruits get

45 POUNDS
(20 kilograms)

weight of gear they carry

L4

Staying Prepared

Training doesn't end with boot camp. Marines train regularly. They need to be prepared for anything.

One training gives soldiers real wartime practice. Each year, the Marines and Navy practice together. They load vehicles and soldiers onto ships. Then some Marines storm the beach. Other soldiers practice firing weapons.

Soldiers who launch guided missiles and fly planes also join the training.

CHAPTER 3

Jobs and Missions

The Marines are a quick-reaction force. They jump into dangerous situations. They battle to take control. Once the major fighting is done, they leave. They let another group, such as the U.S. Army, take over.

Marines are **stationed** on Navy ships around the world. From these ships, Marines can respond fast.

The Marine Corps is part of the Navy. The two groups work closely together.

OTHER MARINE CORPS JOBS

protecting U.S. embassies

protecting the White House

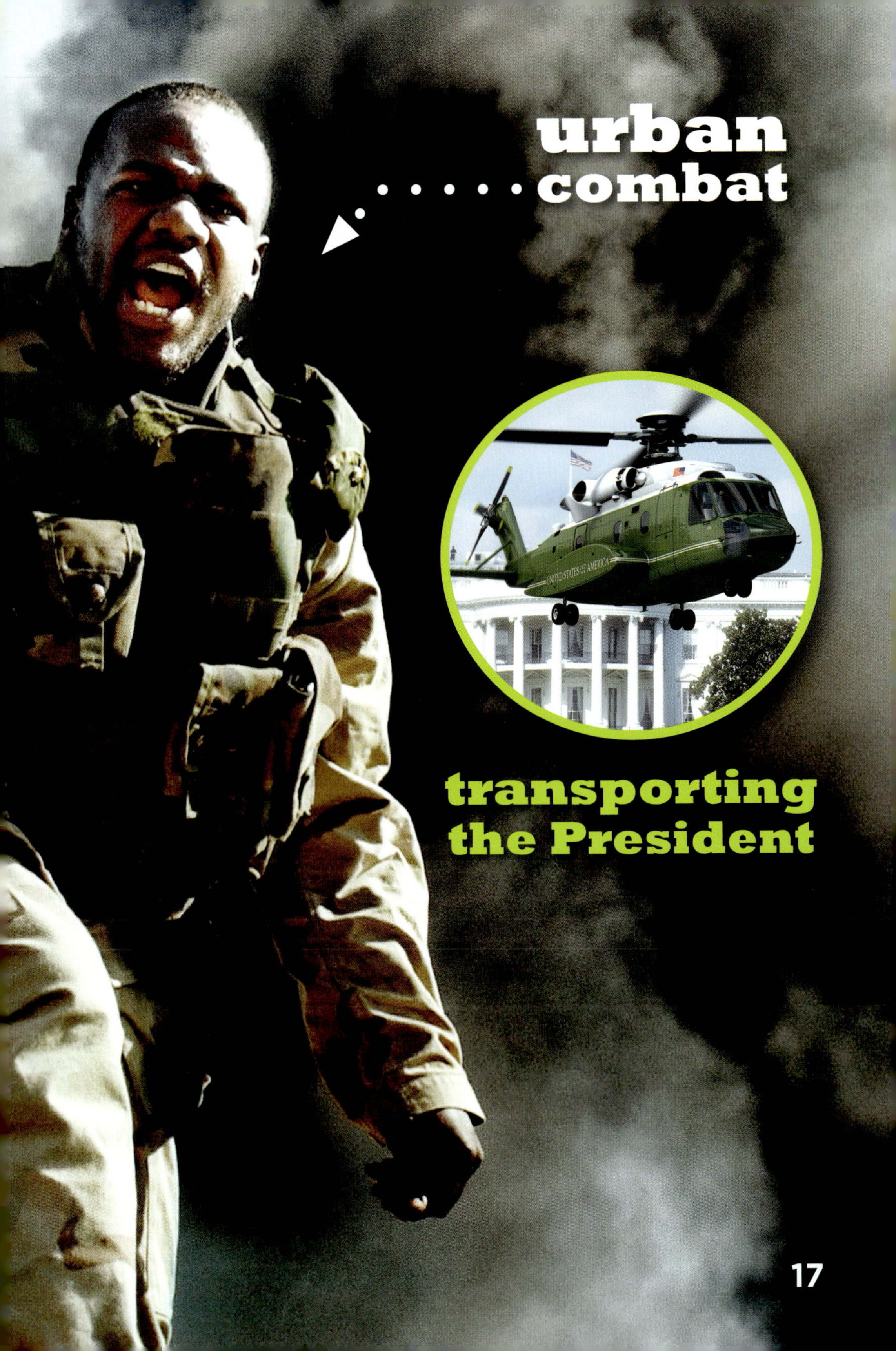

urban combat

transporting the President

United
States

Teaching

Marines don't just help the United States. Sometimes they help other countries. Marines teach other military groups how to fight terrorists. One group helped in Somalia. The Marines were called to help train its army. Marines taught the soldiers to work as a team. They trained them to fire guns and find explosives.

CHAPTER 4

Gear and Weapons

Marines carry a lot of gear. They need it to get their jobs done. They also need gear that protects them. Every Marine has an M4 carbine rifle. They also carry water and meals. In combat, a soldier will carry more than 200 rounds of ammunition.

Marine Gear

BODY ARMOR VEST
HELMET
UNIFORM
RIFLE

AMPHIBIOUS ASSAULT VEHICLES (AAVS)

1 Marines use AAVs to make water landings. Navy ships carry the vehicles.

2 Once the ships get close to a target, Marines drive the AAVs into the water.

3 They continue to drive them on land in search of enemies.

In the Air

Marines are prepared to work in water, on land, and in the air. Marines use many different aircraft to get jobs done. Some crafts carry troops into battle. Others shoot enemies from the sky.

The F-35B is the Marines' most powerful fighter jet. Cameras outside the jet send images to the pilot's helmet. The pilot can see all around the plane.

SOME MARINE AIRCRAFT

AV-8B
Harrier II

F/A-18
Hornet

MV-22
Osprey

F-35B
Lightning II

Always Faithful

The U.S. Marines live by the saying "Always Faithful." They are always ready to serve. Marines travel by air, land, and sea. They are highly trained. And they keep the United States safe.

GLOSSARY

citizen (SIT-uh-zen)—a person who legally belongs to and has the rights and protections of a country

combat (kahm-BAT)—active fighting, often in a war

disarm (dis-ARM)—to make harmless

embassy (EM-buh-see)—the place in a foreign country where an official representative of another country lives

insurgent (in-SUR-jent)—a person who fights against the established government

recruit (ri-KROOT)—a newcomer to a group or field of activity

station (STAY-shun)—to assign to or set in a post or position

transport (TRANS-port)—to carry someone or something from one place to another

urban (UR-ben)—of or related to being in a city

BOOKS

Boothroyd, Jennifer. *Inside the US Marine Corps.* US Armed Forces. Minneapolis: Lerner Publications, 2018.

Grack, Rachel. *U.S. Marines.* Serving Our Country. Mankato, MN: Amicus, 2019.

Mitchell, P. P. *Join the Marines.* US Armed Forces. New York: Gareth Stevens Publishing, 2018.

WEBSITES

The Official Website of the United States Marine Corps
www.marines.mil

United States Marine Corps
www.marines.com

US Government for Kids: United States Armed Forces
www.ducksters.com/history/us_government/united_states_armed_forces.php

INDEX